Southern
MOUNTAIN
LIVING

Southern
MOUNTAIN
LIVING

LYNN MONDAY

GIBBS SMITH
TO ENRICH AND INSPIRE HUMANKIND

First Edition
18 17 16 15 14   5 4 3

Text © 2014 Lynn Monday
Photographs © 2014 as noted on page 176

Published by
Gibbs Smith
P.O. Box 667
Layton, Utah 84041

1.800.835.4993 orders
www.gibbs-smith.com

Designed by Sheryl Dickert
and Melissa Dymock
Printed and bound in Hong Kong
Gibbs Smith books are printed on
paper produced from sustainable
PEFC-certified forest/controlled wood
source. Learn more at www.pefc.org.

Library of Congress Cataloging-
in-Publication Data

Monday, Lynn.
  Southern mountain living / Lynn
Monday. — First Edition.
     pages cm
  ISBN 978-1-4236-3283-2
1. Monday, Lynn—Themes, motives.
2. Interior decoration—Appalachian
Region, Southern. I. Title.
  NK2004.3.M665A4 2014
  747—dc23
                              2013037938

Contents

Acknowledgments

I would like to thank Charles Faudree for his gracious style and kindness to fellow designers. Without his input, I may have never attempted to publish this book. That said, I also owe thanks to all my clients who let me into their lives and homes to make magic. Many I call friends and they have made my life richer. Thanks to my many talented friends who have shared their knowledge with me; I am truly grateful. I also thank everyone close to me who helped through the making of this book, offering love and support when I needed it.

Special thanks to my husband, Wayne, who loves me unconditionally and has always helped pick me up when I've fallen. He is truly my hero.

Love and deep appreciation to my daughter Heather, who makes me laugh; her husband, Paul, who is smart—we respect his input on any subject; my grandson Andrew, who teaches me to be humble; and my granddaughter Grace, who is so like me in many ways—a mini me; my son, Matthew, who keeps my chin up; his wife, Tracy, who keeps style up front; my granddaughter Taylor, who will take over any business and run with it; and last but not least, my daughter Ashley, who keeps me young and up to date with all technology.

Thanks to Madge Baird for guiding me through this first book, and her associates Hollie Keith and Melissa Dymock for helping to create it.

Thank you to Carol Childs, who assisted me with the text.

9

Introduction

Southern Mountain Living celebrates mountain country style with grace and hospitality. Many of the homes in the Southern mountains have been passed down from generation to generation as summer retreats. These family homes have historical character and their own sense of heritage to consider as each generation updates the interior décor. I believe European country manors have lasting style and a timeless lodge look that's right at home in the mountains of North Carolina.

Every mountain home has its own charm and story to tell as well as a divine climate and scenic vistas to celebrate every season of the year. To accomplish this, I mix the formal and the casual in the same space, combining current trends and local treasures with fine art, English and French furniture, antique tapestries, and textiles to maintain a sense of history amid modern comfort and design. I place contemporary elements in a well-worn room or antiques in a sleek setting, always mindful of balance, color, texture, and shape.

This book brings to light the style, grace, and hospitality of living in the Southern mountains. It offers a glimpse, room by room, into a few of my interior designs, making the most of outdoor living and indoor spaces. This is where friends and family come together to make memories and enjoy nature. Come on in and stay awhile.

Porches and Grounds

The Southern mountains of North Carolina offer magnificent views and changing scenery to grace every season with a desirable year-round climate to make living easy, a host of outdoor activities, cultural and civic events to attend, art galleries to browse, sundry antiques shops to visit, and fine dining establishments to please every palate. In the Southern mountains every season is inviting. Spring in bloom is a sight to behold; cool, lush summers draw visitors from near and far; spectacular autumns can take your breath away; and picturesque winters are custom made for cozy fires, inside and out. It's little wonder that virtually every home in the Southern mountains extends the inside living space to the great outdoors.

Whether a rustic porch or formal veranda on a country manor, bringing indoor comfort, style, and character to outdoor spaces can make a porch inviting for entertaining guests, comfortable for quiet evenings with family or friends, and delightful on crisp, early mornings while savoring that first steaming mug of coffee. Porches are a vital part of the best of living in the Southern mountains.

HAPPY HOUR IS ANY HOUR spent on this versatile barn porch at Stillwater Farms on Yellow Mountain. Enjoying early spring weather is a breeze on this custom-designed oversized hickory furniture by Chattooga Woodworks. Turquoise carpet pillows and rich brown cushions in outdoor fabric by Link hone a contemporary mix of textures and tones in this rustic setting. All that's left to do is curl up with your dog or your best friend and drink in the glorious surroundings.

Adding Southern mountain character and historical authenticity to the barn porch, this cowhide-covered trunk is secured with leather strapping and brass hardware, looking natural and timeless against the stacked-stone columns of the barn.

WITH A NOD TO THE PAST and a wink at the present, this well-worn

wicker furniture and down cushions are just the spot. A stacked-stone fireplace takes

the chill out of the air, inviting guests out onto this porch to listen to the waterfall

after a spring rain. Come sit awhile in the sun and share the space with Emma, the

family dog.

AN OPEN PORCH ON A PRISTINE DAY sets the
panoramic scene for luncheon guests, who'll be arriving shortly after
noon. Everyone can be comfortably seated in high-back wicker woven
chairs around a zinc-top table, a neutral backdrop for lively leopard-
print placemats and garden greenery. Out in the open, the gentle
breeze is delightful, and the scent of blossoms and music of songbirds
makes this luncheon a feast for all the senses. The custom swing looks
inviting—a must for that after-lunch nap.

WAGON-WHEEL MIRRORS and an appealing arrangement of wall
pictures add to the illusion of spaciousness. A solid-wood table set with linen napkins
and Russian green glassware is ready for lunch to be served. A driftwood side table
serves as a coffee table and architectural banister lamps add soft light.

Making the most of limited space with five entries opening onto this covered porch,
casual seating is arranged for quiet conversation and intimate dining. What a
wonderful way to spend a lazy summer afternoon with family or friends! White wicker
by Mainly Baskets have cushions and pillows covered in Colfax & Fowler. Custom
drapes in Michael Jasper Smith add warmth and style.

This picturesque barn porch is the perfect place to host a hundred guests for a summer fund-raiser or a few close friends for a champagne toast in the mountains. The client, Robin Visceglia, wanted splashes of color to complement the stacked-stone columns of the porch. Sprays of colorful flowers by Fiddleheads against white linen and bold orange pillows on Adirondack chairs add summer fun and flavor to this elegant formal dinner. This is a perfect night with the horses.

With floor-to-ceiling doors that retract into the walls, this clubhouse porch becomes a unified part of the main building where neighbors, friends, and family can gather together come rain or shine. To brighten any day no matter the weather, a shot of hot pink vivifies the oversized natural wicker furniture from South of Market in Atlanta, while gently pleated drapes soften the stone columns. Coffee tables by La Lune add to the mountain style.

AN ELEGANT SUMMER SETTING

for breakfast, this antique French table has been in the family for more than fifty years. After sanding off layers of old paint and returning it to its rightful provenance, the table now serves admirably alongside restored flea-market French-style dining chairs from the 1950s. For a cheerful centerpiece, a vintage olive bucket holds beautiful blue hydrangeas.

On a lovely summer day, guests can enjoy Southern hospitality while making themselves at home on a tastefully appointed veranda overlooking Lake Glenville. Comfortably seated for conversation on distinctive custom furniture by LaLune, with cushions and pillows covered in outdoor fabrics by Pinnacle, everyone can relax and unwind while the sun dances on the lake.

No welcome mat is needed on this inviting cottage porch in Lonesome Valley. The rocked and shingled walls, hand-hewn pickets and rails, wood-plank window shutters, and solid stone floor say it all: "Come on in!" Adding warmth to the invitation, a slat-back chair, a sporting-dog pillow, and a handmade child's wagon suggest that kids and pets are no doubt also welcome. Amid breathtaking mountain vistas and stunning landscaping, the smallest details often mean the most.

THE SUMMER GARDEN for two on a bright sunny
day is the best place for lunch. The Laurel chairs and rustic table
are set with antique Manhattan glassware from the fifties and
bright yellow napkins. Take a look at the garden's show of
summer colors.

THE PORCH IS LIKE ANOTHER LIVING SPACE.

Winters come alive with roaring fires and summers welcome a view of the gardens. Woven furniture is by Walter Wicker with cozy chenille by Threads. The cherry dining table is set for a casual dinner.

THE SUMMER SLEEPING PORCH is set for a guest to arrive.

The linens and cashmere throw are by Leontine. The white drapes blow in the

cool breeze, giving a fresh feeling.

Four rattan chairs by Warren Fluharty of Asheville are ready to entertain. The mirror from Ainsworth Noah by Ironies has birds and leaves that are perfect for this porch.

FRONT ROW SEATS FOR TWO? No reservations needed! After gathering the last of the season's hydrangeas, just move a couple of handsome wicker armchairs by Restoration Hardware outdoors, lean back and relax on custom-covered cushions by Cowtan & Tout, and watch the sun go down in spectacular full color behind the mountains. As fireflies begin their dance at dusk, brandy is served on a fine silver tray atop an English Rush Stool. Keeping a chenille throw nearby is a good idea in case the air turns chilly after sunset.

Floor-to-ceiling curtains, a Greek garden urn lamp, and an ample walnut-colored wicker armchair make this poplar-sided back porch as warm and inviting as the parlor. Quality indoor fabrics often hold their shape and color as well as outdoor fabrics, as is the case with this lovely window-side curtain from Lee Jofa's David Easton Collection. Completing the mix of textures and eras on this unique porch, a goose-down pillow and cushion by Lee Jofa await your arrival. The cashmere wrap is for curling up under with a good book, first thing in the morning or last thing at night.

SCOOT A FAVORITE CHAIR OUTDOORS

on mild winter days to warm your soul in an Appalachian

sunrise. A plush, oversized pillow on an upholstered chair

adds warmth, style, and comfort to this outdoor setting

against a patchwork of winter vines and a heat-absorbing

stone wall. Think outside the box!

WINTER ON THE FRONT PORCH looks over the mountains as the season rolls in the mist and takes on an eerie look. It truly is a sight to watch the mountain weather as it changes. White rockers with taupe Sunbrella blend so well with the flat logs and chinking.

TO BE INVITED TO DECORATE FOR CHRISTMAS

is always a privilege and gets me in the holiday mood. The front porch is dress out in natural local pine. Adding berries for color, pine cones for texture, and lights is all it takes. Mr. Spencer, the cat, is dressed in his tux and waits for the guests to arrive. Merry Christmas!

Entrances

Entrances make an opening statement to your guests. In the Southern mountains, my designs assure that entranceways are warm and welcoming with surprising mixes of seasonal fresh flowers, vintage vases, perfectly placed mirrors, and timeless antiques, which often are meaningful to the history of the home or family.

Adding a front door with divided light and hanging a large baroque mirror by Maitland Smith over a well-polished bureau fills this entryway with natural and reflected light, making it possible to paint the walls bold black without darkening the welcoming mood.

A custom lamp from Francis Hargrove sheds soft light over fresh-cut white azaleas in a vintage blue-and-white pitcher, a cheerful welcome atop an English drop-leaf table in this simply charming entryway.

THE SUMMER ENTRYWAY

to this clubhouse is open and bright, with a striking custom mirror by Ainsworth-Noah. The impressive ten-foot Spanish chest is the statement piece in the entry, which is both informal and gracious.

A bountiful array of spring flowers in a vintage blue-and-white porcelain urn is doubly stunning reflected in a hanging oval mirror with custom antler by Stag Ridge. The antique French chest adds charm and warmth, as do the hanging lanterns, which glow softly when lit. Welcome!

The inviting entrance to this log cabin reflects the autumn season in tune with the turning leaves outside. An old pottery jug, some bright fall flowers, a few leather-bound books, and an understated lamp make the entrance feel cozy, while the seventeen-foot drapes, handsome French cabinet, and leather riding boots make it feel more like a country estate. The landscape oil painting by Sheri Erickson duplicates looking out the window, with vibrant fall colors welcoming one and all.

AN ENGLISH CHEST AND BLACK FOREST MIRROR, facing,
make the most of small spaces with a lot to say. Notice the flight of ocelot carpeted
stairs reflected in the mirror and the walking sticks ready to take a walk.

This custom home on Lake Glenville
is rustic and elegant as the entrance
hall shows tall silver vessels with horn
handles that hold cuttings of nature.
Bark mirror and a fruitwood console
add warmth and texture. The wall
sconces are by Dana.

THE ENTRANCE TO THE DINING ROOM

boasts a French chest and painting of snow and pine trees,

which is a great setting for a Christmas poinsettia placed

in a coal hod. An antique cigar box and cutter gives the

feeling of days gone by when after-dinner men settled in

the drawing room to have a cigar. The lamps were a find at

Edgar Reeves of Atlanta, Georgia.

Great Rooms

The great room in the Southern mountains is the center of the home and reflects the style and history of the family. I will take you on a journey of scale, balance, texture, shape, and color. The traffic pattern of the house, the floor plan, taking in the clients' needs. How do they live? How do they entertain? The great room should be comfortable and flexible. I love volume, and most of the great rooms in the mountains have vaulted ceilings, large beams, and massive stone fireplaces, requiring a designer's eye to keep the proportion in balance. The ambiance should be warm and welcoming, charming and very personal. When working with a collection of antiques, I like to give a fresh, updated approach. Maybe it's reupholstering a chair with a contemporary fabric or placing a new lampshade on an old lamp, giving it better proportions. All must be arranged to create a room that flows naturally with Southern mountain hospitality.

MY CLIENT MOSS ROBERTSON wanted a sofa he had seen in the movie *The Thomas Crown Affair*. With that said, I custom made a pair of sofas with a traditional Ralph Lauren wool plaid and a contemporary fifties mindset. The client's wish came true. The bookshelves and coffer ceiling give this room a timeless quality. The linen velvet in green gives texture to some antique chairs. Moss added Ralph Lauren's burled coffee table, giving a modern look to tufted English leather chairs. The walls add warmth. Antique books, art, and accessories give an acquired look while current books, art, and accessories keep it fresh. One night Moss called me while sitting in his new room with a friend. He wanted to say how much he loved his room. This is why we design . . . to please the client.

This was my second home for Alec and Doreen Poitevint, with a collection of European antique furniture, which Doreen loves so much. Adding just enough Black Forest accessories will create a country house. The towering stone fireplace frames a French circa-1850 Aubusson tapestry. A pair of custom antler chandeliers falls between beams, adding drama and light to this room. I added fresh printed linen by Lee Jofa for the windows and modern wing chairs. The sofa is by Schumacher with down cushions and a tone-on-tone herringbone pattern, keeping it full of comfort. The French side chair flanking the sofa is in misty green linen mohair. This is the life, owning a country house in the tranquil Southern mountains. No reservations needed.

THE CLUB AT CHATTOOGA RIDGE wanted

the great room to be neutral. I stained all the doors and beams dark walnut to contrast against the light walls and floor. A custom-made hunt board with birch inlay stands smartly beside the central fireplace. Oversized wicker chairs and sisal rugs provide the texture needed in a neutral palette. The window treatments are Ralph Lauren fine linen. The sofas are custom in natural taupe linen. The game table is stained dark hickory by La Lune. We have garden urns with custom wood tops as side tables. The seating is both intimate and casual. Giving a natural flow to this room lends itself to private parties or larger events.

JOHN AND SHARON BISSELL wanted a light and airy feeling to their country cottage. Spring-inspired design brings this room to life. Custom sofa and lounge chairs in pale green provide comfort. The window fabric in Schumacher cream and green flanks grass-woven shades. A custom wood cabinet painted cream and distressed houses the pop-up TV, and the coffee table was given new life with cream paint. With a stump-inspired side table, porcelain dragonfly lamp, and custom pillows with garden critters, this room feels like spring.

Penny Johnson wanted a formal great room but still in keeping with Southern mountain estates. The strong beams anchor the massive windows. A generously sized hand-forged chandelier by Ashore Design that is beautifully scaled adds perfect proportions. The grand French buffet with antique gold baroque mirror reflects the summer flowers outdoors, which is repeated in the linen window treatments and custom pillows. Small glass tables in a zigzag pattern are given new life as a coffee table. Bringing the room all together, this bold-colored rug is an antique Heriz by Bounds Cave.

THE CABIN AT BALD ROCK is nestled in the woods and has an old worn feeling, as if it had been passed down through the family, but in fact it is new and therefore needed some history. As a designer, I have to set the stage for Dave and Kerrie Bauer to feel right at home. The colors of nature were all around this cabin. Sometimes nature dictates the direction I must travel to get the outcome that is needed. Taking our cue from nature, Kerrie and I pulled a fabric from Schumacher with a light background and many shades of green for the windows. We did not want the cabin to feel dark, so adding a light-colored Aubusson rug with a hunting design fills the cabin floor with forest animals. Rustic design has a history of its own, so we set on a path to have local artisans make the hickory pieces to give credibility to this cabin. Loveseats and lounge chairs by Charles Stewart call you to sit awhile, put your feet up, and listen as the fire crackles. Stop and take a moment to reflect about your own history that you made today.

Oftentimes, when a new room is added onto a house, it looks out of character. Such is not the case in this great room with its old hand-hewn beams and two handsome lanterns that give the room an authentic aged look. The sofa and armchairs are upholstered in textured linen and the country French dining chairs are detailed with Don and Alacia Rhame's monogram.

Across the room, a stacked-stone fireplace with a painting by John James Audubon displayed over the mantel gives a nod to nature while the French buffet anchors the room. An oversized mirror and heirloom family plates are displayed with great attention to detail. The coffee table was a side table cut down to just the right height. This room's attitude is all about Southern hospitality, but wait! Alacia will play the piano and make her guests feel special with her enormous talent.

This mountain lake house has views from every room. The great room with angled wood ceiling and architectural beams is massive yet cozy. The stone design is strong, softened by painted horizontal boards, giving it a lighter, charming feeling. A pair of English sofas by George Smith helps develop a feeling of a country retreat. The family crest painted on a leather trunk used as a coffee table adds personal history. Experience is best to determine the size and weight of a chandelier. I have placed it in the center of the room for maximum lighting.

A bright and airy cabin with painted walls and red accents is the background for a collection of French fishing creels, and by adding antler mounts and snowshoes, you have cabin provenance. I always feel like I am just back from a walk by the creek in this great room. Get the fishing pole; the fish are jumping! What's for dinner tonight? Fresh trout!

JAMES WEST BOUGHT THIS HOME to give it love, and love it he did. Some things are better left undone than done poorly. This is a pristine summit country home, kudos to James. The great room is massive with historically inspired painted walls and stained ceiling, which creates a canopy of gray and green dancing light. The panoramic view is one that delivers the seasons right into your great room. Architectural trusses have visual personality. At this level of craftsmanship, I added to the mix iron and leather furnishings to carry the space. James, with a discerning eye, bought an earth-toned Hajijalili Tabriz rug. I could not have been more pleased. It correlates with colors right outside the window—stone and grass with a nod to fall when it shows up.

$\mathscr{Sitting}$ $\mathscr{Rooms}$

The sitting room is a place I find that clients need, a room to start the day or retreat to, a personal spot for reflecting their interests and heritage with personal collections and, of course, comfortable furniture. The guest sitting room is a place that feels like home, a place people can put their feet up and give a nod to the great day they had in the mountains restoring their peace of mind.

Original art over the mantel by Dennis Campay from the John Collette Fine Art Gallery. Cashmere pillows by Brenda Beye. Zebra rug by Bounds Cave of Cashiers.

A SMALL RUSTIC LIBRARY is just the spot for the homeowners to have an after-dinner brandy in front of the fire or to write a note on a Ralph Lauren desk. The custom window treatments are cashmere plaid by Ralph Lauren. The chairs flanking the fireplace by Lee Jofa are upholstered in linen. Take a look at the family pictures and the trophies. This is truly personal space. It is a cozy place to retreat from the chilly mountain evenings.

This sitting room has multiple uses, serving as an overflow space for guests or for reading or watching a favorite movie. Take a look at a hostess collection of coffee table books. Step out onto the balcony, look at the mountains, and take in the clean air. This is a small room with a vaulted ceiling. I dropped in a custom antler chandelier by Stag Ridge, which hangs between the beams, and a Black Forest stag mount fills the space over the window. A pair of Louis XIV chairs upholstered in modern damask give the room an updated look. The French commode (circa 1700–30) and the garden vessel lamp with custom shade stands smartly in the window. I used many patterns in this small room, and I have found that when doing so, using two colors will help. Another way I can use multiple patterns in the same room is by keeping all the colors in the same tonality.

A
ROOM
OF HER
OWN

Chris Casson Madden

MIRROR by DESIGN
THE PERFECT COUNTRY COTTAGE
HOME
PROVENCE THE ART OF LIVING
The COUNTRY GARDEN

PETER AND SHEP'S GUEST SUITE

is Southern hospitality all the way. With a sixty-inch television and a fully stocked bar, Peter and Shep set out to give their guests a treat. They wanted a place that would rival a five-star hotel. Refined, established, and exclusive was the feeling, as if it was always there waiting for the guest to enjoy. Custom sofa, lounge chairs, and ottomans are upholstered in textured-pattern chenille by Quadrille. The faux furs add warmth for guests. Barstools are by Guy Chaddock. Take a look at the etched glass dated 1706 found in a good friend's shop, Skip Ryan of Ryan & Co. Custom window treatments are by Schumacher.

Whether for dining or reading, this room has a view of the lake and mountains. Sometimes the dining room is not used for dining, so to rethink this room I gave it a purpose with little effort. The table became a library table and the dining chairs pulled up to work at the table. The room is now the favorite place in

the home. It is quiet and has breathtaking views of the mountains and lake. Custom window treatments in Cowtan & Tout with Houles trim frame the views. I designed a graceful custom antler chandelier by Stag Ridge to illuminate the English-inspired pedestal table.

AN ALCOVE in a hall outside two bedrooms is a guest sitting room. Spring is here; you can hear the birds singing and smell the morning dew. The day starts in this room with a custom mirror by Chad Collins, sofa by Brunschwig and Fils, and cane-back French chairs with down seats in pale blue linen. A pair of French side tables, circa 1930s, came from the Country Home, owned by good friends George and Eddie. The pair of matching lamps came from Ainsworth and Noah, owned by my friends Hal and Winton. I called engineer Gordon Gray to make a grid so that wall treatment I wanted for this space would look like lattice, giving the feeling of spring but not like any I had ever seen. I tacked nail heads, shiny nail heads, directly into the dry wall to create a pattern. Like any good designer, I tried it at home first. The upholstery tacks went in and stayed. The large country French chest with pine cones and pods was a find in Atlanta at Ainsworth and Noah, and adding a modern lamp updated this chest, giving it new life.

CUSTOM BOOKCASES STAINED DARK

with white-painted shelves is the perfect place to display a collection of blue-and-white porcelain and antique books. This Adirondack bookcase was custom made by Chattooga Woodworks, created just for this space, giving a sense of history. The detail of the dramatic, low, log ceiling captures the feeling of a quaint English dwelling. Edward Ferrell chairs and sofas covered in silk velvet give a rich ambiance to this charming log room. Notice the hunt board, a La Lune look-alike, over which is an antique wooden industrial mold (that has to be within one-sixteenth inch of perfect, requiring impressive craftsmanship).

THE WINE SALON is a comfortable, intimate room where you and your closest friends can share the finest of your collection of wines. This room started out quite dark. Walls, ceiling, and floor were stained. Not wanting to change the stain, for it had great provenance, I set about adding life and light to this room. A pair of 1930s channel-back chairs are covered in natural linen with legs and trim painted soft yellow. Two nesting tables, repurposed as a coffee table, provide just the spot for a glass of wine. A contemporary chest by Kravets is painted a pale yellow to give plenty of color to the room, and adding a light-colored patterned rug gives it a modern edge. Cheers!

This once was a dining room and now we have created a whole new space transforming it to what is now a rustic anteroom. Antique turned lamps with custom lampshades cast a light upon the George Smith tufted leather reading chairs.

Kitchens

The recipe for a Southern mountain kitchen is one part country look and one part tailored function. Beams give a kitchen an aged feeling, but of course antiquated appliances need to be updated and modernized. Kitchens are the heart and soul of a home, and as a designer I need to respect the family and friends of my clients. I give them room to move around and yet make it easy to prepare food, creating a happy marriage between form and function. A well-designed kitchen requires preparation time to assemble the key ingredients: appliances, cabinets, counters, flooring, and lighting must all work together as one.

Southern cooking is so much better when the cook is happy, so before starting any kitchen, I always check with the cook. We have so much fun in the kitchen with the flops as well as the triumphs of our culinary endeavors. Southern mountain cooks often follow old family recipes passed down from generation to generation, recipes filled with memories.

For this client we designed a kitchen with both form and function. White on white provides the background for the colors he loves so much. A La Cornue stove in Provence blue and counter stools in red leather add colorful sophistication to this kitchen. The chandelier is Tiffany's (love the old style) and the glazed country cabinets add age to the brand-new kitchen. Making dinner for two in this Bear Lake home is Southern mountain living at its best.

THIS KITCHEN WAS A RENOVATION

job that began with a serious look at the short, hunter green cabinets. We considered whether to install new cabinets or just re-paint the old ones. With that said, we decided to take the existing cabinets to the ceiling, adding shadow boxes with puck lights at the top to give the kitchen both style and volume. Then my client and I set out to find the perfect color for the cabinets, and we did just that. The color works perfectly with the Caesarstone countertops, which have a Carrara marble look but with less veining. One of my favorite ideas to come out of this renovation was the suspension of pots and pans on a rod with hooks as a pullout system just below the cooktop in the island, making cooking just a little bit easier and more fun.

THIS LAKESIDE KITCHEN combines stonework with

granite, giving it a strong mountain aesthetic, and adding detailed

painted cabinetry helps soften the effect. A large island is an oasis

where friends and family gather, providing front-row seats for the

cooking show to come. Counter stools with a rustic finish and

ultra-suede seats are by Guy Chaddock. This kitchen inspires my

client to cook, bringing joy to all meals. Add a dash of stone to a

slab of granite, sprinkle in a few painted wood details and stainless

accents and you have a sure-fire recipe for memorable meals.

COUNTRY FRENCH NEUTRAL

describes this renovation and how the client wanted to prepare meals. It was a must that everything she needed was at her fingertips. Granite counters and new appliances helped achieve the goal of working efficiently. Adding a wall of small tumbled marble subway tiles and a French iron fireback fills the space above the stove. Did you know that firebacks were invented centuries ago to keep the backs of hearths warm? The shadow box displays the client's collection of plates and figurines, beautifully personalizing her kitchen. Now she is prepared to stimulate taste buds and delight palates.

Dining Rooms

Dining Southern mountain style is both welcoming and delicious, from linen napkins and fine crystal to family china and silver. The way I see it, there are no rules for casual dining. But first you must know all the rules before you can break them. Southern homes have mastered the art of entertaining in the mountains, taking the formal and dressing it down. Make your table your own mix of plates and glassware. I like to add texture, candles, and art objects; details that will stimulate the senses and enhance the flavor of the food. Adding color sets the mood of the season or holiday, allowing guests to take a moment at the table to feed their visual appetite before the first bite. The Southern hostess always takes the time to care; it is second nature to gracefully fill the room with music and conversation. This is the rhythm of the mountains.

EARLY MORNING BREAKFAST in this cabin
is set with Galax leaves and white china. The French napkins
in cotton twill give guests the order number for the eggs or
pancakes that Carrie will be serving. On the lighter side,
a bowl is set for fresh fruits of the season. Rhododendron
leaves are placed in an antique stone garden planter to
give texture and visual interest, and the table and chairs
are custom made by Chattooga Woodworks, adding an
Adirondack feel. The rustic chairs are dressed up with
brown-and-green-velvet-striped cushions by Schumacher.
What a wonderful way to greet the day.

LIGHT BREAKFAST and mimosas served beside new French doors that open onto the garden make this morning repast a must. Adding to the inviting appeal of this breakfast nook, custom-designed bookcases flank the channel-back banquette I designed. The painted country French chairs look fresh in casual dressmaker cushions with inverted pleats. The client's old pine table was just the size needed to seat six. The sun shining through the French doors brings in a warm glow and takes the chill out of the morning mountain air.

LUNCH IS SERVED! A seasonal fruit plate is all you need to accompany a glass of Prosecco Italian sparkling wine. The glass-top table with an iron base makes this light and airy room with vaulted ceilings feel fresh. Custom parson chairs in taupe linen are trimmed with a green welt to add contrast and sophistication, while two country French chairs upholstered in the same green stand smartly beside a French buffet. The two multicolor glass lamps found at C. K. Swans in Highlands, North Carolina, are just perfect for framing the original lily pad art by Mary Pratt, a Georgia artist. By adding wall brackets and French majolica plates, everything comes together with charming detail.

The spring cottage dining table with custom French chairs infuses charm in this small intimate dining room, which opens onto a covered porch. Two antique-finished chests provide balanced symmetry and practical storage space. A collection of bird prints adds grace and drama to the room, making this truly feel like a Southern mountain cottage. The place settings are casual yet elegant. This is where a classic combination of whites works so well with entertaining. Keep it simple in small spaces.

MICKEY AND DIANA PALMER LOVE TO ENTERTAIN

in their second home in the mountains. Diana will surprise you with New Orleans

cuisine and a night of food, wine, and laughter to remember. Fall is full of color just

outside this home perched high on a ridge. Color, color, and more color fills the view

for dinner guests. Leaves, gourds, and pumpkins on the table add to the fall palette,

while unexpected objects like quill boxes, antler mounts, and a woven collection of

small Native American baskets add interest. Custom-made dining chairs are covered

in Marvic fabric, and a casual mix of stemware gives sparkle to the table that I custom

designed. The old Oushak carpet is placed at an angle to draw your eye into the room

and out to the view. Diana found this vintage textile Swedish quilt that I had framed.

The antique carved oak Flemish cabinet anchors the wall beneath the hanging. A pair

of Canadian Louis XV chairs came from the Quebec region. Dining among the fall

trees captures the essence of the mountains.

THIS TABLE IS SET

for a casual lunch with woven placemats. Spode plates with linen napkins bundled in dragonfly napkin rings—still linen but not so formal. The use of brown and green glasses and blue hydrangeas from Don's garden add further to the casual feeling. A four-paneled screen painted with hunting dogs adds to the country nature of this room.

This Christmas luncheon is charming and whimsical, set for family and a few close friends. The dining room was added on, having once been a porch, and the panoramic view makes dining a feast for the eyes. The only thing I wish I could change is that it would have snowed this day. The placemats are casual but the color of Christmas, the plates dressed out in Christmas salad red and green. The table is country French with a rustic finish and the high-back leather chairs with nail-head trim are from Guy Chaddock. An antique French cabinet and hunt board add provenance. A bronze chandelier hangs in the vaulting—see the deer dancing! The drapes by Schumacher frame the windows and add warmth. The dressing is about to be served. *Bon appétit*.

An early dinner at the farm is both casual and elegant. The hand-carved candleholders with deer are Black Forest, giving European harmony to the English table and chairs as well as to the French country host and hostess upholstered chairs. I custom designed the window treatments in fabric by Kravet with small pleats and iron rods. Woven placemats and a basket of fruit add texture and color. The horse grazing on spring grass just outside the windows is intoxicating to watch. Mountain living on a farm is both healthy and rewarding. The view of the mountains and animals grazing is simply the best.

Bedrooms

The bedroom should be quiet, comfortable, and serene. Stretch out and feel completely relaxed, put your feet up, and glance out the window. Dusk is giving into the night. Your guests come to see you; give them the royal treatment. Make the bedroom a place to remember: a good bed, pillows (I like goose down), and great white sheets with a hint of bleach and lavender. Add soft cotton, cashmere blankets, or a down comforter, for the mountains are cool at night, and a matelassé to pull over the sheets. On a tray by the bed, place water and a book of thoughts; guests should be happy to have you as a friend. The right lighting is a must, so if they choose to read in bed, they will appreciate that you have given them the light to do so. A side chair, chest, bedside tables, and a bench will make them feel at home.

Often when I have guests, figuring out what they might like to have is a mission. When my sisters came to my home to stay for the weekend, knowing that they all loved sweets, I filled a basket with candies in each bedroom. Some guests like after-dinner drinks; a tray of mini cordials will work. Chilled champagne is nice to welcome them, and wine, flowers, candles, and fresh towels are a must. An iron, ironing board, and a blow dryer are nice appliances to provide. Soap, shampoo, and cotton balls added to the bathroom give a personal touch. Make a checklist of their anticipated needs. This is what it means to come to the mountains and be a guest; it is truly Southern hospitality.

The master bedroom in this small cottage has a fresh feeling. A custom headboard with nail-head trim frames the cozy chenille fabric. The dust ruffle is made as a dressmaker's skirt with stitched-down box pleats and button details are a smart touch. Painted cream walls and furniture with antique finish set the stage for the embroidered drapes and pillow shams. An antique French engraved collection depicting men and their trades hangs over the bed and down the side wall, giving a dash of the masculine side. I sold the French collection out of my own home, and another designer owned them before me. All designers love nice things and love to share those nice things with others.

This is a small guest room with a vaulted ceiling. My client wanted a king-sized bed; I made space by placing custom wall brackets on each side of the bed to serve as nightstands. The wall-bracketed swing-arm lamps left the nightstands free for a glass of water and a book. The colors in this room, gray, white, and green, keep the color palette simple. Gray woven-grass shades and a linen dust ruffle, a white chair and bedding, green printed drapes and euro-shams move the colors around the room as if it were a painting. This room is a great place for family or friends to sleep well.

This bunkroom is for the grandkids, and I had three hickory beds, three stools and a chest custom made in the mountain look. The box springs where exposed, so we custom covered them with the same fabric as the drapes and shams. By adding simple bedding, this room is always ready for the grandkids. Take a look at the geese; they look like they are floating on the walls. Clear shelves work well to give you this look. The Adirondack-style chest is by Chattooga Woodworks and the mirror is by Stag Ridge. An iron lamp by Indus Design and turtle shells by Nature add interest, bringing the outdoors in. Simple and smart.

This guest room for the daughters has a feminine yet grand feeling of staying in a country French château. A rustic iron bed in updated fabrics set out to do just that. When mixing patterns, prints, stripes, checks, and paisley, use the same color palette, which in this case is soft and serene. The room has an angled ceiling with a fan, which presented a problem when the client wanted a canopy, so I set out to give her what she wanted. Shortening the blades of the fan kept them from hitting the canopy, and mitering the boards of the canopy creates the illusion that the ceiling is flat. The glass-bead trim by Kraft's looks like evergreens, adding one more feminine touch. The skirted dressing table is needed for the client's daughters when they come to stay. This room provides a personal sanctuary.

CUSTOM TWIN-BED HEADBOARDS are fashioned after the English wing chair with welt and tufting in wool. The antique rug over carpet was needed to anchor the beds. The large-check fabric on windows and pillows are by Schumacher. The dust ruffle is Ralph Lauren paisley with wooden beads as trim. The fabric on pillows and upholstery is in embossed fern velvet. This room has a warm glow about it as if the sun is shining, even on a rainy day in the mountains.

A king-sized bed in this guest room
is imposing with a lattice-inlayed
headboard and turned corner posts,
making a great first impression.
Dressing out this commanding
bedroom, the hall mirror with antlers
was given new life as art décor, drawing
the eye up to the high windows. French
engraving plates of the countryside
add charm while filling the wall behind
the headboard. An antique cherry
desk with mirror serves as a dressing
table. A small writing desk flanking the
bed becomes a nightstand. Drapes in
checks with a wide border at the hem
and detailed trim by Samuel & Sons
visually balance the room. Breathtaking
sights of the Southern mountains are
just outside this bedroom window.

This lake view guest bedroom is dressed out in fern fabric. A desk and bench by La Lune add needed weight because of the strong beams.

THE TOILE MASTER BEDROOM

in red and cream with small checks is a classic.
Having done this room some years ago, it
reminded me that French toile lives on. I once
heard a quote that if you do not have a toile
bedroom in the South, you need one. The room
off the bedroom overlooks a waterfall. This
sitting room is where my clients read and listen
to the rhythmic sounds of nature awakening and
falling asleep in the quaint and very Southern
mountains.

A MASTER BEDROOM full of treats from solid
wood lamps to a cane-back bed custom made by my
nephew Jeff Collins, owner of Chattooga Woodworks.
I love the fully upholstered bench that sits in the window.
The collection of bird prints from George and Eddie at
A Country Home make this bedroom feel like you are a
part of the pulse of nature.

This wood bed is grand with botanical prints leaning in over the top edge of the headboard. Yes, we secured them to the wall to create the illusion of leaning. Notice that the bedside table lamps are actually wheels. As designers, we are always looking for something different, and this room took to novel touches quite well.

A CABIN MASTER BEDROOM with light-colored fern-printed window treatments keeps the room looking fresh and welcoming. The bed, painted black and distressed, makes a commanding statement against the wood walls. A pair of chests with onyx tops are just the right height and add symmetry to the room. Rustic white lamps on the chests provide contrast, and the green wicker side chair is by Mainly Baskets. Don't wake me in the morning; I am sleeping in, because I can.

This small bedroom feels large, and the proper placement of furniture and accessories contributes to the illusion. The custom daybed is fashioned in farmhouse style, with lily-of-the-valley embroidered pillows adding a nice touch. Tramp-art wall brackets hold white plates, and the custom antler bracket by Stag Ridge (Chad Collins) provides height. Placing the desk going into the room takes your eye across the space. The distressed green chest with leaf details and a faux log lamp and birds bring the outdoors in.

This bedroom has all the elements of a guest room you can be proud of. Sometimes the architecture of a room can determine what needs to be done and how best to do it. Painted beams extend down the wall to sixty inches, so that is the height of the custom headboard. Edwin's Covey is the name of this fabric with birds and ferns by Scalamandre. Mixing cotton with silk checks gives the room a feeling of luxury, and the French cabinets hold additional linens. Custom cane barstools work well for handling suitcases, while two large French upholstered chairs are perfect for lounging. A desk with bear details adds charm, and the fern artwork is hung at an angle because of the room's architecture.

Baths

Bathrooms are the most private places in one's home; they need to function for clients and guests. I love giving the bathroom that clean look and then adding jewelry, mirrors, faucets, and lighting to reflect sophistication and personality. Whether the decision is for rustic, glamorous, or a cottage look, there are many expressive possibilities to consider, such as custom cabinets or furniture for a vanity. The simplest way to make a bathroom cohesive is to design one element in the bathroom with a strong dominant feature, perhaps adding windows or a stone wall.

Even in an older home, where you want to maintain the integrity of the age of the house, you still need to update the functionality. This small, intimate space can make or break a home. Many great lines offer fixtures and mirrors that will take you back to any era. Sometimes a bathroom is already great, and all it needs are the accessories to give some personality.

THE DESIGN OF THIS bath is in the architecture, which is crisp and clean. In so keeping, fresh evergreen potpourri provides a truly mountain scent. A couple of trout pictures and clean towels are all this bath needs for finishing touches.

THE SECOND BATH

in this home with the same aesthetic adds a linen shelf to an otherwise dead space. Subway tiles surround the shower, adding to the clean and fresh look.

Wood walls with doors and trim painted white are so easy on the eyes! The glazed cabinets create a painted furniture feeling, and metal fern light fixtures placed on the mirror add a touch of nature. French doors open invitingly onto a small hickory balcony. Grab your robe and walk outside into the fresh air to take a look at the glorious mountain morning.

A small bath requires a designer to think outside the box. The wall sconces I wanted to use would not work flanking the mirror in this bath, so I added them instead to the side, providing both light and visual interest.

This master bath was a total renovation, and the views were what made it a complete success. Take a look at the shower built for two and the windows. The tub feels like you are sitting and taking your bath on the lawn.

My client wanted a bath that was both rustic and romantic. Painted and glazed cabinets with quartz counters and hammered silver sinks give an updated, glamour-meets-the-mountains allure.

Working with clients while their homes are under construction allows a designer to incorporate an idea like a stone wall for the bath to enrich texture and atmosphere. Using a narrow worktable as a vanity adds character, and together with a bark mirror, wall sconces, and a well-placed basket creates the perfect rustic powder room for a mountain home. Think outside the box!

Powder rooms should be treated like any room in your house: they must relate to your own interests and taste. Using an old pine chest, a small desk lamp, some artwork, and two engaging antique wall sconces gives this powder room all the personality it needs.

Afterword

have given you some insights into how we live in the Southern mountains. Southern hospitality is alive in the details of the homes and the natural surroundings. When your soul beats in rhythm with nature, you soon find yourself happy and content to be creative in your own home.

Always taking colors and textures from nature, I advise clients to choose colors from trees when they ask what color to paint the exterior of their homes, and they will never make a mistake. The mountains whisper of gentle days and sleepy nights. The home takes on the life of all who live inside, a casual personality with plenty of provenance. From the basket that was made locally to your grandfather's rocker, feelings are what make your home yours. As designers, we bring this all together to give a design that works. We are all about the details of needs and desires.

Spring is in the air; smell the flowers and listen to the bees as they fly back and forth gathering nectar. The birds have returned, singing their many songs. The air is fresh, filled with the scent of flowers. Clients are busy getting ready for the coming days when their guests will arrive. Flowers are beautiful, adding to any room, giving it life. Open the drapes, wash the windows, and ask a great designer to help you with a spring color story for your home. Life is about change, and spring is the best time to welcome in the new.

Quiet winds rustle through the trees all summer with the sound of rain pitter-pattering into the night; as day breaks, the sun climbs high in the sky to cascade the dance of light through branches and leaves, bringing a new day's warmth. Tennis, golf, biking, climbing, or just a walk—all will renew your soul. The home brings family and friends together for more of that Southern hospitality. We need to make the home an arrangement that meets the needs of all who enter; the perfect balance.

Summer turns to fall, and the mountains take on the splendor of color. We gather on the porch wearing sweaters and jackets to marvel at the mountains' variety of colors. As designers, we love fall, taking that season's colors all through the home: an arrangement of branches with brightly colored leaves, adding placemats in orange and a few pumpkins; an orange cashmere throw by Hermes adds a nice touch.

The leaves blow away, giving a nod to winter days ahead. Inside mountain homes, roaring fires are lit; faux fur pillows and throws add warmth as family and friends gather for the holidays. I aim to have the homes ready for the Christmas holidays. Natural garlands and wreaths with berries, pine cones, and white lights set the stage for a mountain Christmas experience. Let it snow, let it snow.

Shops That Are a Must

ACORN BOUTIQUE BRANDS

445 Main Street
Highlands, NC 28741
866.526.8008
oldedwardsinn.com/
shopping/acorns-
boutique-brands

A COUNTRY HOME

5162 Cashiers Road
Highlands, NC 28717
828.526.9038
facebook.com/pages/
A-Country-Home
/160661603953872

A VILLAGE GARDEN

Cashiers, NC 28717
828.743.6114

AINSWORTH AND NOAH

351 Peachtree Hills
Avenue, Suite 518
Atlanta, GA 30305
800.669.3512
info@ainsworth-noah.com
ainsworth-noah.com

BASKETWORKS

560 Highway 107 South
Cashiers, NC 28717
828.743.5052

BEAR PAW DESIGNS

572 Highway 107 North
Cashiers, NC 28717
828.743.2004

BOUNDS CAVE

337 Highway 64 East
Cashiers, NC 28717
828.743.5493

BUMPKINS

9 Cashiers Commons
Cashiers, NC 28717
828.743.5497
bumpkins-cashiers.com

CATBIRD SEAT ANTIQUES

551 Highway 107 South
Cashiers, NC 28717
828.743.6565
ryanandcompany
antiques.com

CHATTOOGA GARDENS

91 Valley Road
Cashiers, NC 28717
828.743.1062
chattoogagardens.com

CHATTOOGA WOOD WORKS

69 Flash Point Drive
Cashiers, NC 28717
828.743.3483

CJ BROWNHOUSE

10 Chestnut Square
Cashiers, NC 28717
828.743.0097

CONSIGNMENT MARKET

12 Chestnut Square
Cashiers, NC 28717
818.507.3325
consignmentmarket
cashiersnc.com

DOVE TAIL ANTIQUES

252 Highway 107 South
Cashiers, NC 28717
828.743.1800